Pieces of Grace

And What They Mean

Dream
Street Lullaby
The Answer
Fallen Star

LITTLE DOZEN PRESS

Pieces of Grace (And What They Mean)

Published by Little Dozen Press
Windsor, Ontario, Canada
http://www.littledozen.com

"Dream," "Street Lullaby," and "The Answer" originally performed live with Soli Deo Gloria Ballet.

Cover photograph by Deborah Thomson; cover design by Becky Thomson. Copyright 2010

ISBN: 978-0-9739591-9-2

Pieces of Grace

And What They Mean

Dream
Street Lullaby
The Answer
Fallen Star

by Rachel Starr Thomson
and Soli Deo Gloria Ballet

LITTLE DOZEN PRESS

Table of Contents

Part I:

The Pieces

Dream

I.

As I lay me down to sleep
As I close my eyes
I am carried into a dark, deep place
I descend into a dream.

Mist slips all around
Wisping haze, faded signs pointing the way
To an ancient town . . .
To a place I almost remember.
To a place I think I know.

In the fog, fire-wrought gates take shape
Forbidding and familiar.

II.

The fog is full of phantoms and half-memories
Splintered songs floating from beyond the
gates.
And I remember
That this was once my home.
Here is my innocence
Here is who I nearly was.

I should go back, but the gates are closed to
me.
And only the living may return
And the life that is in me is not life
The light that is in me has gone out
Are these chains on my soul?
I cannot crack this death.
I cannot find the way.

III.

All grows dark.
I stand outside the gates of ancient town.
On the other side, two trees stand together
Branches tangled, entwined.
One tree is all my longing.
The other is all my death.
I look through the gates to the ancient place.
A garden I cannot enter
A presence I may not approach.

Shadows swirl around me
Voices in the night.
One offering salvation—
The other a voice I know.

Here in the darkness,
I hear my own voice.
I am my own friend.
I am my own enemy.
I will take all I want,
I will sell myself to do it.
Other voices echo mine,
Demons or shadows or friends,
While the gates remain closed,
And I am still chained.

And another voice cries from beyond fire-
wrought bars
"Do you remember now?
Do you remember what you should be?
I'll save you from yourself."

Shadows swirl around me
Voices in the night.
One offering salvation,
But I am afraid.

IV.

And then the voices fade away
And I hear a song, unsplintered, high and
clear.
The mists begin to dissolve in light,
And I see the gates are open
Tangled tree branches have formed a cross
And around it, chains lie shattered.

Behind me the song grows stronger
And I turn to see the sun
And a throng of singers walking toward the
garden
Scents of innocence and glory blow forth
And I lift my voice and sing along.

Amazing grace
How sweet the sound
That calls to me
To come.

Street Lullaby

I.

Stop. Hush. You in the street.

Hear the feet rushing? Mouths speaking? Noise building? Stress pounding?

Hush.

Overwhelming, overbearing, overtiring world. Everything building as you stand in crowded places in this moment utterly surrounded.

Hush.

Hush.

Close your eyes for a moment. Listen well. Let us bring you a street lullaby.

II.

Cast your cares. Throw them away. On the only One you really need—listen to the music of ancient peace, standing in crowded places in this moment utterly alone, looking up toward heaven.

Stand in the peace of God and look up—reach for grace, here in the crowd, here in the waking sleep of a lullaby.

III.

And are you now waking? Wake still in the Father's peace.

And are you now going? Go in his grace.

Do you now turn back to face the world, the noise, the building, overwhelming, speeding pressure of crowd and sound and need?

Go in the arms of love.

Go in the dance; wake in the lullaby; now; always.

You are safe in the song.

The Answer

Based on Isaiah 42

I.

O God, we need you now.
We hunger and we thirst.
We tear each other apart.
We murder and enslave
We turn a blind eye.

We are bruised and breaking
We are ready to fall.
Our light grows dim.
Answer us, O God.
Give us a word.

I.

(The Answer)

"Behold my servant, whom I uphold,
    my chosen, in whom my soul delights;
I have put my Spirit upon him;
    he will bring forth justice to the nations.
He will not cry aloud or lift up his voice,
    or make it heard in the street;
    a bruised reed he will not break,
    and a faintly burning wick he will not
    quench;
    he will faithfully bring forth justice.
He will not grow faint or be discouraged
    till he has established justice in the
    earth;
    and the coastlands wait for his law."

II.

O God, we need you now.
We hunger and we thirst.
We turn a blind eye.
We are blind, we are poor, we are broken.

Can we be saved?
Can we be transformed?
Will you rescue us from our poverty?

II.

(The Answer)

"Thus says God, the LORD,
>who created the heavens and stretched
>them out,
>who spread out the earth and what
>comes from it,
>who gives breath to the people on it
>and spirit to those who walk in it:
"I am the LORD; I have called you in
righteousness;
>I will take you by the hand and keep
>you;
I will give you as a covenant for the people,
> a light for the nations,
>to open the eyes that are blind,
>to bring out the prisoners from the
>dungeon,
>from the prison those who sit in
>darkness."

III.

O God, we need you now.
We hunger and we thirst.
From the deserts to the mountains
From the islands to the cities
We look for hope, springing forth
We wait for you.

III.
(The Answer)

"I am the LORD; that is my name;
Behold, the former things have come to pass,
    and new things I now declare;
    before they spring forth
    I tell you of them."

Sing to the LORD a new song,
    his praise from the end of the earth,
    you who go down to the sea, and all that
    fills it,
    the coastlands and their inhabitants.
Let the desert and its cities lift up their voice,
    [let them] sing for joy,
    let them shout from the top of the
    mountains.
Let them give glory to the LORD,
    and declare his praise.

Fallen Star

"Oh God, help me to believe the truth about myself,

no matter how beautiful it may be."

for Debbie

Christmas 2005

She fell.

We watched her fall: a fallen star. We called out to her but she could not hear; we reached out, but she slipped through celestial fingers—drawn by the twinkling lights of Earth. She did not want to stay with us, she said; it was dark in the high places; dark and cold; she wanted to leave.

We watched her from above. By the time she reached the streets, her light had all but gone out. Only sometimes late at night, when the sun had gone down and the Earth was darker than the heavens had ever been, we could see it: a tiny, steady glow still burning in her heart. We missed her then. We wished she would come back to us.

* * *

She showed up in the city early one morning, a bedraggled alone child. She wandered the sidewalks until morning, when she found a group of other pseudo-runaways outside a coffee shop.

A young guy wearing a black tuque and a big jacket, with half a day's growth on his chin, noticed her. "Hey," he said. "I'm Dodge. Haven't seen you around before."

She attempted a smile. "Astrea," she said. "Looks like a nice place." She motioned toward the coffee shop with her chin. Her hands were too cold to take out of her pockets.

"Here," he said, "I'll buy you something."

She turned and looked down the street, where the sun was shining through buildings, its light crisscrossed by wires and traffic lights in never-ending succession. Her feet were itching to follow the light, to get out of here. But her stomach told her to follow him. Coffee wasn't breakfast, but it was better than nothing.

She nodded and followed the little group through the dark doorway. There wasn't much light in the shop. The floor was dark tile, marked here and there with cigarette butts. Small tables and wire chairs ringed the room. Black-and-white photographs hung in frames on the wall. She stepped closer to one so she could see it, and recoiled. It—all of them—were pictures of impurity: the exaltation of lust, the fall of love. They repulsed her and fascinated her all at once.

The loud music playing in the back had the same effect. Her blood started to race as the music filled her with excitement, with fear and uncertainty and a strange sense of power. She felt suddenly as if life were a river, flowing inexorably to some unknown fate, and she had just been caught in it for the first time.

She turned away from the pictures as Dodge thrust a cup of coffee into her hands. The smell of it was inviting.

They all stepped back outside, and the morning chill stung her face. She lifted the cup to her lips and let the steam warm her. Dodge looked her way from over the top of his own drink.

"So," he said, "where'd you come from?"

She lowered her cup and stared down at it for a minute. Her fingers looked cold and small, clutching the drink as if it was a shield. He had no idea. She couldn't tell him, of course. *Even if he believed her—which he wouldn't—how could she describe the sky?* She shrugged.

"I . . . left home," she said.

"Wasn't what you wanted, eh?" he asked.

She took a sip of coffee. It burned her tongue.

"Right," she said. The liquid seemed to make her a

little stronger. She thought of the family above and the Presence that had commanded them to burn. "I had father problems."

Dodge laughed. "Who doesn't?" he asked.

They talked a little more, and the group dispersed: Dodge to work, a long-haired kid home to a cellar, the others to their various lives. She spent the morning wandering through the riverside park, watching the seagulls pick at garbage and scraps of bread. Smokestacks across the river painted the sky with poison, and the air grew increasingly colder as the day wore on. Chunks of ice floated down the river. She watched them for a while, and then went off to find new sights.

She found her new friends again at night, when the world of the city was transformed. The night was strange and exotic. The night taught her things. On the rare occasions that she stepped outside, she was relieved to see that the summer smog clouded out the stars. She imagined they looked on her reprovingly, but she didn't care. Resolutely she didn't care.

It didn't take her long to make a life for herself in the city. She found a job, met people, carefully chose places to be that would distract her from herself—more important, that would distract her from the sky.

As time went on she realized that, inside of her, things were frighteningly dark. The light that had always been a part of her seemed to be going out. She denied it at first—it was a part of her, it couldn't go out. It wasn't possible. If it faded, if it went down a little . . . well, that was fine. The colder the fire within, the more she was able to fit in with the city world.

But the light continued to fade, until it started to scare her. She began to seek out light—something that could rekindle her own soul. Not healthy light, not daylight, for the sun was nothing but a great star intent on burning past her careful exterior and exposing her to the world. She sought out the garish, fluorescent lights that men use to disguise darkness. The places she frequented pumped light, used it to dazzle and blind. They were nothing but darkness in masquerade, and it didn't take her long to learn that.

Frightened, she began to plunge deeper into darkness. Maybe, when she'd reached the darkest place she could find, the light inside her would react by flaring to life again. In truth, she was becoming afraid of lights. They reminded her of the sky, and she was sure the sky wanted nothing to do with her. In time she learned to dislike even the city lights. When she was outside she would rush from place to place with her collar pulled high around her neck and her eyes cast down, desperately avoiding the sky. They were out there somewhere. They were watching. Condemning. Shining judgment down on her. She grew to hate the stars.

She would never admit—not to her friends, who would have thought she was crazy, not to herself, not to anyone—that she missed them.

* * *

She woke up in a panic. It was early morning before the sunrise. Her hand went automatically to her belly, just beginning to swell. Her chest heaved with emotion . . . relief, fear, crying. She was fine. The baby was fine.

She lay back in bed and blinked away tears. It was too dark to see the room, but voices and memories crowded into her head. She wished she could shut them up, turn them off. There was a letter on the bedside table, sitting there somewhere in the dark. She didn't want to remember what it said. This was not a good time to face being alone.

It was the loneliest hour of the night, and her defenses were down. A sudden longing for the sky loomed up in her. Once, a very long time ago, she had been able to pretend that she belonged up there. She hadn't . . . but at least they'd allowed her to stay. At least they'd loved her. And it was better—better to be a pretending star than to be here, now, facing everything, with a deadness where she'd once had light.

She knew she was giving into emotion and she'd regret it later, but she didn't care. She wanted to see the sky again. She wanted to look the stars in their faces and dare them to say what they thought. She stumbled out of bed and pulled on her ratty brown coat, shoved her feet into her slippers, and banged her way out the back door. The air was cool and fresh. She was living out in the suburbs, where the city lights and smog didn't rule the sky. Every night she had avoided looking at the sky. Now she determinedly turned her eyes up.

She couldn't see them.

Not one.

She'd heard the neighbours talking just the other day about the amazing clarity of the sky, about all the stars they'd counted with their children. But she was blind to them. Despair crashed in hard on her heart. She knew it wasn't a matter of cloudy skies. The smog was in her eyes, just as the voices and music were in her head, drowning out peace, just as the images and scenes and memories were in her heart, tearing her slowly to pieces.

She sat down on the step, buried her face in her hands, and cried.

* * *

A year had come and gone since the day Astrea had come to Earth. She was walking around the city, waiting for contractions to begin so she could hail a cab and go to the hospital. She could have waited at the house. Probably should have. But there was no one there, and she couldn't stand the emptiness and the silence. At least, out in the cold of the city, she could listen to the traffic and watch the people and pretend that someone cared.

She looked up briefly, searched the sky. There was nothing there but a few clouds and the ribbed exhaust of a plane that had flown past a little while ago. The blue was beginning to fade to grey; night was approaching, but the city lights that reflected off the snow wouldn't allow the sky to turn black.

She'd feared this city once; then loved it; then hated it. It didn't deserve any of her passions now. She knew it too well. It was an old friend whose character she'd come to despise. It was, at least, constant. The others had gone, but the city stayed. And stayed. Its noise and its smog and its hardness carved themselves in her heart where they would always stay.

The wind stung her face as freezing rain bit into her cheeks. She turned her head away from the wind and saw him, less than a block away. She thought . . . yes, she was sure it was him, though she could only see his back. Dodge. He was back in the city, and he hadn't called her, hadn't even let her know that he was there.

Suddenly there were angry tears in her eyes, and they stung as badly as the rain. He couldn't just stand there like that, back turned to her, as though she didn't exist and nothing she was going through was his fault. She wouldn't allow it.

She took a step toward him, and then another, and another, and her fists clenched as she walked. The wind blew her hair into her face and pushed her forward. Her high-heeled boots beat a bitter tattoo on the sidewalk. She willed him to turn around and look at her, but he only continued to stand with his hands in his pockets, talking to someone, even laughing. Laughing, while she was out in the cold. She walked faster.

His companion left the sidewalk and crossed the street, and suddenly Dodge began to walk away. Her stomach tightened; a near-panic gripped her. *Not now. He can't leave. Not now. Not again.*

She started to run, ignoring the wind and the slush and the traffic. Her eyes were only on him, and he was getting away from her.

Her ankle wrenched, and she fell. Somehow

she had stepped off the curb into the gutter. Slush trickled down the inside of her boot: numbing the pain or accenting it, she wasn't sure which. She pounded her fists on the pavement and cried. Wailed. He was gone. He hadn't even looked back.

No one seemed to see her. No one stopped to help. Her ankle throbbed, and within her the baby kicked. Any time now. The baby could come any minute, and she was in the gutter, wet, muddy, hurting, alone.

She didn't know how much time passed before she pulled herself up again. The wind had picked up, lashing against her mercilessly. It drove her to seek shelter in a door frame, hobbling across the sidewalk in search of protection from the weather. She huddled in close to the building, turned, and looked up. It wasn't a deliberate looking up, just a reflex.

But she saw it. A single star. Blazing out, more

than usually large and bright, a mysterious beacon in the sky.

Calling her.

Somehow the star was calling her. She couldn't quite hear the name it used. She had forgotten it so long ago that she couldn't make out the sound of it now, but she knew the name meant *her,* a deep inner her that hadn't really lived for a long time. Perhaps it had never really lived.

She could not take her eyes from the star. It was almost hypnotic. On every side, the noises of the city seemed to fall silent. The sky, at first a cloudy grey, darkened so the star shone even brighter.

She took a step toward it, and suddenly the city passed away from beneath her feet and she was in a great wide space somewhere. Tears again came to her eyes, but they were not now of anger. The light of the star seemed to expose all of her secret sins and fears, and she stood helpless and vulnerable before it—yet she could not resist its pull. Once again she took a step toward it, and now she found herself on a hillside, looking down on faraway lights. The air was warm. The wind and its stinging rain had gone, replaced by a deep and holy stillness.

Suddenly the sky was alight with stars. A beautiful tension filled the air; the vibration of a thousand celestial harp strings. They all were looking on her, urging her to return to them. Their light bathed and tended her. She trembled under their ministration even as she pulled away from it, ashamed and afraid to let them touch her.

Their song was high above her, the words beyond her comprehension, but she knew they were calling her higher—and she knew she could not go. Not if they welcomed her with open arms. Her soul was too dark; her wounds past healing. There was no ladder to heaven that could lead her back home.

The star that had fallen could not go back again.

She lifted her eyes, and the star that had drawn her separated itself from the others by its sheer brilliance. It seemed to hover directly over the hill where she stood. She gazed at it for a long time, and then it dawned on her—very suddenly—that the star was a sign. Its light was shining on this hill for a reason.

Whatever she was looking for was not above her, in the sky. It was beneath her. In the hill.

Cautiously, she began to move toward the steep edge of the hill. The dirt under her feet was loose, and it rained away beneath her as she inched forward. The path was steep, but she could move along it if she crouched; and she clutched at roots and long bits of grass to help steady her descent.

A sudden noise, close by her feet, startled her so that she nearly lost her balance and slid. Heart pounding, she gripped a handful of dry grass and waited. The noise sounded again, and this time she recognized it. A cow. There was a cow, somewhere in the darkness below her.

She peered through the gloom, and finally saw what she'd missed before: a hole. The entrance to a cave. Its darkness had made it nearly invisible before, but now the opening yawned below her, and she dropped down into it. Her feet hit hard-packed earth, and the smell of straw and manure assailed her. She was in a stable, carved into the hillside, what seemed like millions of miles from the city and her life on earth—but very close, somehow, to the heavens.

A rocky crag obscured the way into the stable; around it, some sort of candle or small lamp was burning. It cast strange shadows in the entryway where she stood, lighting the rock in flickering gloom.

She rounded the corner slowly, her heart pounding. Every sense seemed heightened as she moved. The smell of blood and sweat mingled with animal smells in the air; she could hear something stirring. A feeling of vastness, greater even than what she remembered in the sky days, threatened to overwhelm her. She stumbled as she came around the corner and dropped, trembling, to her knees.

She found herself looking into the dark, exhausted eyes of a young girl. She sat in the straw, her back against the rocky wall of the stable, clutching something in her arms. She regarded Astrea warily, too tired to move, yet with a glimmer in her eyes that spoke of strength and determination. The look of defensiveness faded as the girl took in Astrea's appearance. The girl moved slightly and attempted a smile. Her grip on the bundle of rags in her arms loosened slightly, and as she lowered her arms, Astrea saw the face of a newborn baby nestled against the girl.

A stable.

A girl.

A *baby* . . .

She knew this story. Her eyes grew wide as she looked at the child. The air was full of voices, full of the vastness of space, full of eternity. She was on Earth, but in the face of the child she saw the Ancient Heart of the Universe—something older, greater, more terrifying than the heavens. She dropped her eyes, let them focus on the straw and the blood-and-manure-streaked floor. She felt the deadness and darkness inside keenly. It threatened to swallow her from the inside just as the child's overwhelming presence threatened to destroy her outwardly.

She wanted to shine. Tears slipped from her

eyes. Her fingers curled into the palms of her hands, and she closed her eyes, focusing on the dead place inside. Desperately she wanted to rekindle the flame that had once been hers, but she could not. It was gone. Dead. Cold. She sat in the Presence, the same Presence that had filled the heavens where she was born, and she shamed herself and dishonoured the child by being something so far from what she was meant to be.

The girl in the stable spoke. Her voice was soft, questioning, but Astrea could not understand the words. Still, the voice drew her eyes up again, and once more she looked at the child. The tiny boy had turned his head toward her, and his eyes were open.

Astrea gasped as she looked into the perfect, sky-coloured darkness of his eyes. There, deep within them, starlight shone.

The heart of starlight, the source of starlight,

was in his eyes, and it seemed to her that he offered it to her—a gift.

For the first time she realized the starlight had never been hers. She thought she had extinguished it, but she hadn't, she couldn't, because it didn't belong to her. And if it was to burn in her again, it would have to come as a gift from the outside. From the child. Hesitantly, tears streaming down her cheeks, she raised her hand and reached out to touch his head.

* * *

She couldn't make out the words. Voices were buzzing low around her, and someone was grabbing at her arms. She opened her eyes for a moment, and the city lights made her wince: red and blue lights, whirling around her. Ambulance. She was being lifted onto a stretcher. She gasped as a pain deep inside her drew her hand to her belly. They had arrived just in time.

She tried to search out the sky as they began to move the stretcher toward the ambulance. She smiled. The stars were shining down on her, thousands of them, millions of them, regardless of the smog and the city lights. They were smiling. And deep within her, an answering flame flickered. It warmed her from the inside even as the winter cold bit at her outwardly. She swallowed back tears as a star shot across the sky, leaving a wake of light that formed a pathway across the Milky Way.

She had found the ladder to heaven, and inside of her, the Gift-Light was burning again.

Astrea closed her eyes as the roof of the ambulance blocked out the magnificent sky. She was still smiling, a secret smile, all to herself. It would be many years before she took that path. She could not leave until her child was grown and safe. But her light had been rekindled. Even here, even on Earth, she would fellowship with the sky.

Part II

What the Pieces Mean

About Meaning

Life, some say, is meaningless. But I don't believe that. I believe everything means something. Only the author can tell us what is meant by a particular thing. Since I wrote the particular poems and stories in this book, I can tell you what they mean —or at least, what I intended them to mean.

So if you have been struck by something read previously in these pages, or your curiosity is aroused, or you just want to hear more, read on.

What "Street Lullaby" Means

"Street Lullaby" was written to be spoken into noise. We wanted to reach out and grab people who are busy and overwhelmed, and make them pay attention for a minute.

Our world today is constantly making noise. It can be overwhelming. Traffic, talking, footsteps, coffee machines, ringing phones, dinging computers, music over loudspeakers, announcements, chatter, noise, and noise, and more noise.

Added to the physical bombardment is the spiritual noise that haunts us: our dreams and fears, hopes and failures. The further we move away from childhood, the louder both kinds of noise get.

When it's performed live, the stanzas of "Street

Lullaby" are interspersed by lullabies which Carolyn dances. Lullabies are sung by parents to children to remind them that they are loved and protected, that someone cares for them; to inspire beautiful dreams and especially peace. Adults need this too, because we are still children on the inside.

The invitation of "Street Lullaby" is to come to God the Father and enter His peace. Paul, one of the earliest Christian missionaries, opened his famous epistle to the Romans with the greeting, "Grace to you and peace from God our Father and the Lord Jesus Christ." He closed it with the words, "Now the God of peace be with you all. Amen."

In the King James Version of the Bible, the Hebrew prophet Zephaniah wrote this beautiful description of God as He gives peace to His people: "The LORD thy God in the midst of thee is mighty; he will save, he will rejoice over thee with joy; he will rest in his love, he will joy over thee with singing."

"Street Lullaby" is our invitation to you to enter the presence of a peaceful Father who sings over those He loves.

But peace has two facets. One is internal—the way we feel. The other is external—our position with God. (Paul's epistle to the Romans is a powerful message about external peace with God. He argues that we are not at peace with God because of our wrongdoing, but God is reaching out to us with grace and forgiveness through Jesus Christ. It's brilliant, beautiful, and well worth reading.)

This external peace is unreachable unless we are delivered from ourselves. And that leads into our next piece of grace—"Dream."

What "Dream" Means

In "Dream," a young woman falls asleep and descends into a world just as real as the physical one—but she has never confronted it so clearly before.

In her dream, mists swirl all around. Through them, she catches a glimpse of an iron gate, its bars carefully wrought by fire. The gate is closed, but she is drawn to it. As she comes closer, memory stirs. The gates guard a place she has seen before.

What lies beyond the gates might be a garden, or it might be a town—a lonely place, or a community. She is not sure. But her conviction grows stronger that she has been here before. In fact, she was born beyond those gates. This is where she comes from.

Longing grips the Dreamer to return home, but she realizes that the gates will not open to her. Her origins were in innocence and true life, and she has lost both. She was born free, but now chains bind her. She has never admitted this in the waking world, but here in the dream it can't be denied.

She realizes there is a Presence beyond the gates as well. Someone she wants to return to—but does not dare approach.

"Dream," as we perform it, is in some ways an allegory. In other ways it is not. It is what we believe is real. If we could see our spirits, we would find ourselves in the same position as the Dreamer. We would find that we are enchained, and the chains are of our own making.

The garden and town beyond the gates represent Eden, the fabled garden where mankind first disobeyed God and turned to evil. In a sense, we all have our origins in Eden. We all go through the process of falling from innocence, of embracing various kinds of death, and of slowly enslaving ourselves. Paradise is closed to us. We cannot get back in.

As the Dreamer mourns the loss of her ancient home, shadows swirl around her, and she begins to hear voices. Two voices. Both offer her hope.

One voice offers her salvation. It is a strong, frightening voice, and it comes from inside the gates. It promises to come to her and free her from herself, but the Dreamer is afraid of it.

The other voice, she realizes, is her own. She has her own best interests at heart. She will do everything and anything to bring success to herself— but in the process, the chains will only grow tighter. The gates will remain closed.

Other voices join her voice, but the Dreamer

cannot tell whether these voices are friends or enemies, angels or demons.

This too is reality. The voice of God, through His Son Jesus Christ, offers us salvation if we will trust Him to save us. But this means letting go of our own attempts to save ourselves, and it means turning away from many things we may have embraced so we can embrace God instead.

On the other side, we promise ourselves everything. But we find ourselves unable to keep such promises without digging ourselves deeper into our holes—further from the garden, further from who and what we were meant to be.

Beyond the gates, the Dreamer sees two trees that have twisted themselves together. "One tree," she says, "was all my longing. The other was all my death." These represent the trees found in Eden according to the Bible (Genesis 1-3). One, the Tree of

Life, gave humans the ability to live eternally. The other, the Tree of the Knowledge of Good and Evil, represented humanity's first act of self-promotion in rebellion against God—and in that act, humanity's fall from paradise.

But the Dreamer sees that the trees have twisted themselves together and formed a cross with their branches. The gates are opening, the mist is clearing, and she hears voices singing in the sunshine about something called "amazing grace." As she listens and begins to sing along, her chains fall free, and the way into the garden is opened to her.

The Bible teaches that God, desiring to restore people to relationship with Him despite their evil-doing, rebellion, and lost innocence, sent His Son Jesus Christ to make reconciliation. Jesus accomplished this by dying on the cross. He took the consequences of one tree—the tree that represents our rebellion and wrongdoing—on Himself. And He gave us the fruit of the other tree—the Tree of Life. We could not pick that fruit again, but He could, and He gives it to us as His gift.

John 3:16, the Bible's most famous verse, says it clearly: "For God so loved the world, that he gave his only Son, that whoever believes in him should not perish but have eternal life."

And that is what "Dream" means.

What "The Answer" Means

We all know the world is a mess—and when it comes down to it, most of the mess is our fault. People kill other people, even helpless infants, the elderly, and the weak and ill. People misuse resources and cause famines and shortages. People cheat others and refuse them justice. People are selfish and greedy, so other people suffer. People wage unjust and senseless wars. People turn a blind eye and a cold heart.

"The Answer" is about our mess. It is a prayer for God to help us, even though we are struggling in a trap we laid for ourselves. The first part of each stanza is a simple prayer for help.

The second part of each stanza, the answers, are quotes from the ancient prophet Isaiah. They are recorded in the Bible in Isaiah 42. These are prophecies about a man God will send to bring justice and mercy to the earth, to open prisons and make the blind see. When Jesus Christ walked the earth, he read Isaiah 42 and claimed he was the one who would fulfill it.

We don't yet see the fulfillment of these answers, but we believe Jesus Christ is alive, that He will return, and that when He does, He will reign for a thousand years, bringing true justice for all.

"The Answer" is a reminder that we should hope for this return. It is also a reminder that until Jesus does come back, it is our responsibility to act as He would act and to bring justice and mercy as much as we can to our fellow man.

What "Fallen Star" Means

"Fallen Star" is the only piece in this book which we have never performed live with music and dance to accompany the story. I wrote it years ago as a gift for someone dear to me.

The story is pure fantasy. I do not really believe that stars can come down in human form. But I hope it says some true things about people. We are all fallen in one way or another. We were all born for something better. We are all, in one sense, more beautiful than we know—and in another sense, we are all more lost than we know.

The stable scene which Astrea comes across is, of course, the birth of Christ. It's the story told every Christmas in songs like "Silent Night" and "Away in a

Manger." The child in the scene is Jesus Christ, the Son of God. Astrea realizes that her light, her true identify, her purpose, are all in Him. Even though she has given these things up, He can give them back to her. And He does offer them back.

The same is true for us. We are not what we should be. We are lost and guilty. But Jesus offers us forgiveness and new life. The Bible says of those who trust Jesus, "Therefore if any man be in Christ, he is a new creature: old things are passed away; behold, all things are become new."

That is what the story means.

Finding Meaning

Earlier I wrote that everything has meaning, and if we want to know what that meaning is, we must ask the Author.

If you are intrigued by pieces of grace in this book, pick up a Bible. That collection of stories, poetry, prophecy, and letters was inspired by the Author of Life. Start reading with the Gospel of John or the Epistle to the Romans.

If you can't find a Bible, e-mail us at solideoballet@gmail.com. We'd be happy to send you one.

Rachel Starr Thomson

Soli Deo Gloria Ballet

About Rachel Starr Thomson
and Soli Deo Gloria Ballet

With the exception of "Fallen Star," the pieces in this book were written for live performance with Soli Deo Gloria Ballet, a professional-level Canadian ballet company that uses dance, narrative, and the creative arts to explore ancient truths and bring glory to God.

Rachel Starr Thomson is a writer and co-director of Soli Deo Gloria Ballet, along with dancer Carolyn Currey.

Soli Deo Gloria Ballet is based in the Niagara Region of Ontario and tours throughout the year, presenting short pieces and full-length ballets in churches, schools, festivals, conferences, and more,

For more information, visit us on the Web:

Rachel Starr Thomson
http://www.rachelstarrthomson.com

Soli Deo Gloria Ballet
http://www.solideoballet.com